Letter Sounds
to Help Parents Help Their Children

Not a Workbook, but a Work-With Book

Peggy L. Forster

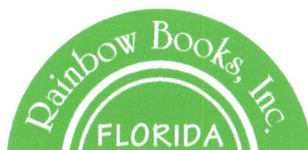

Rainbow Books, Inc.

FLORIDA

Introduction — Read Thoughtfully

Learning that my five-year-old grandson, Gavin, was having trouble mastering the letter sounds launched me into a search for help on the Internet. Nothing I found was what I had in mind to help him. Having been a first-grade teacher before "Sesame Street" began, teaching letter sounds was part of my resumé. So — teach!

This is not a workbook — it's a work-with book.

It's designed for a parent, a grandparent, or older sibling and the child to work together, one-on-one, to name the pictures and to complete the exercises that follow each set of pictures.

To make the letters easy to find, the pages are in alphabetical order, except for the vowels, which are at the end. This does not mean you must work from Bb to Zz, in that order.

- **Begin with the easiest sound — Mm**. A lesson plan for **Mm** to help get you started follows this introduction.

- **Let the child choose the next letter** — maybe the beginning of his or her name. You can put your child's picture on his or her page. (Gavin's photo is on the **Gg** page.)

- **Stop! before interest lags.** Ten minutes might do it! End by choosing the letter for next time — maybe the first letter of the name of a sibling, friend or pet.

Vocabulary building — It will happen, considering that at least 250 words are needed to identify pictures and to complete the exercises.

The name under each picture is there to clearly identify it with the letter sound on that page. Calling a horse a pony or a rabbit a bunny isn't a mistake, it just calls for thinking of another name that begins with the same sound as the other pictures on the page.

The main purpose of this book is to acquaint the child with the sounds of the symbols of the written word.

Above all, this should be a fun time — something the child can appreciate as being done **with** him or her, not **to** him or her.

Enjoy!

Peggy L. Forster (aka Mamaw)

Lesson Plan for Using "Letter Sounds to Help Parents Help Their Children"

Before beginning letter sounds, the child should be acquainted with the alphabet and the fact that it is the letters of the alphabet that form the words that tell the stories we love to read. Okay? Let's get started!

To begin, turn to the Mm page. Identify the letter **Mm** (big **M**, little **m**) at the top of the page and demonstrate the sound it stands for: **mmmmmm**. The mmmmmm sound should be made clearly and cleanly without a vowel sound attached. It is mmmmmm — not muh! Other letter sounds that can be demonstrated with a single sound are fffff (not fuh), hhhhhh (breath only, not voice, not huh), llllll (not luh), nnnnnn (not nuh), rrrrrr (not ruh), ssssss (not suh), vvvvvv (not vuh), zzzzzz (not zuh).

The letters b, d, g, j, k, p q, t and w can't be elongated to demonstrate their sound, so a word is the model for the sound.

Now, back to Mm —

- Have the child name the letter **Mm** and make the **mmmmmm** sound.

- Ask the child, "Do you see anything on this page that begins with that sound — **mmmmm**?"

If the child can identify one or more, YAY! Help the child identify all images on the page, then go to the exercises on the facing page.

But, if there is a reluctance to respond, point to the milk and ask, "How about **mmm**ilk. Does milk begin with **mmmmm**?"

- Have the child say "milk" two or three times, then ask, "Do you hear **mmmmm** at the beginning of **mmmm**ilk?" (The child's head should be nodding yes.)

- Stay on the word milk until it becomes more **mmmm** than ilk.

- Follow the same procedure for each picture on the page.

- Review the page by naming each picture one more time.

Now go to the exercises on the facing page. Answers are at the bottom. Freely use your charade, pantomime and acting skills to offer clues.

Follow the same procedure for each letter.

Bb as in bubble

balloons

ball

box

banana

books

Begin to think of other Bb words you know.

What do you put soup or cereal in?

What do you ride that has two wheels?

What do you hit a baseball with?

What do men wear to hold their pants up?

Which picture **does not** begin with the **Bb** sound?

ANSWERS: bowl; bike; bat; belt; mittens

Cc

Cc doesn't have a sound of its own.
It can have the Kk sound, as in

cat

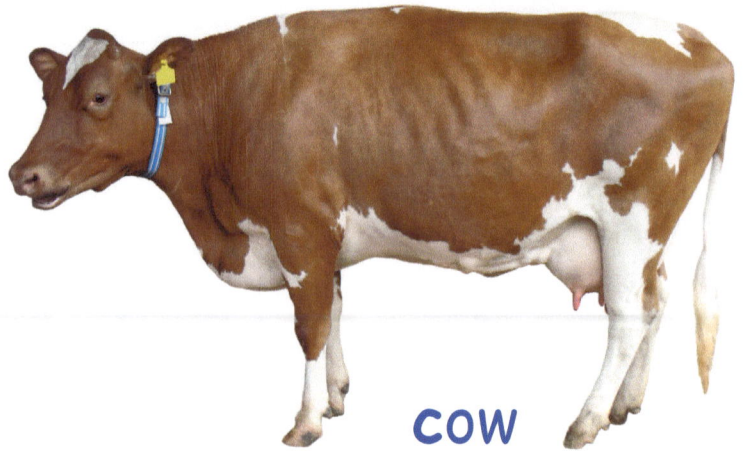

cow

cup

corn

Can you think of something sweet you like to eat that begins with the Kk sound of Cc?

ANSWERS: cookies, candy, cake, cupcake

Or Cc can have the sound of Ss as in

celery

cereal

circles

Do you know a girl's name that starts with the **Ss** sound of **Cc**?

Who lost her glass slipper when she ran from the palace?

ANSWERS: Cindy, Cynthia, Celia, and more; Cinderella

Dd as in daddy

dog

doll

deer

duckie

Do you know more Dd words?

What can you do with a shovel?

What do you like to do to music?

At a swimming pool, you might d _ _ _ _ into the water.

If something tastes really good, you say it is d _ _ _ _ _ _ _ _ _ .

Do **both** of these pictures begin with the **Dd** sound?

How about these two?

Ff ffffff

family

fork

fox

fish

fence

Find two pictures below that begin with the Ff sound.

You see a lot of trees growing in a **f** _ _ _ _ _ _.

Who hurries to put out fires? **f** _ _ _ _ _ _ _.

A lot of soft, cuddly animals are covered with **f** _ _.

When you lose something, you look until you **f** _ _ _ it.

Which picture **does not** begin with the **Ff** sound?

ANSWERS: fork and fish; forest; fireman; fur; find; dog

Gg as in giggle

girl

Gavin

goose

goat

Go for more **Gg** words —

Do you like to play video g _ _ _ _ _ ?

What are you chewing? Bubble g _ _ ?

You can grow vegetables or flowers in a g _ _ _ _ _ _ .

ANSWERS: games; gum; garden

More about Gg —

Sometimes the **Gg** sounds like a **Jj**, as in

giraffe

gingerbread

Hh

hhhhhh (breath only, no voice)

house

hammer

hamburger

horse

How about more words that begin with the Hh sound?

When you're sad, you're not h _ _ _ _ .

In the winter it's cold. In the summer it's h _ _ .

A kite can fly very h _ _ _ .

Eat a good lunch so you won't get h _ _ _ _ _ .

What do you wear on your head when you ride a bike?

What else can you wear that starts with the Hh sound?

What would you put these gloves on? The answer starts with the Hh sound.

ANSWERS: happy; hot; high; hungry; helmet; hat; hands

Jj

as in jump

jelly

juice

jack-o-lantern

jelly beans

jump rope

Just keep thinking of the Jj sound —

Can you think of a friend's name that begins with **Jj**?

Pick **two** pictures that begin with the **Jj** sound —

What is this dessert that jiggles? It starts with the **Jj** sound.

ANSWERS: Joey, John, Josh, Jacob, Jennifer, Jan, Joy, and more; jacket and jeans; Jell-O

Kk as in kick

kitten

kangaroo

kitchen

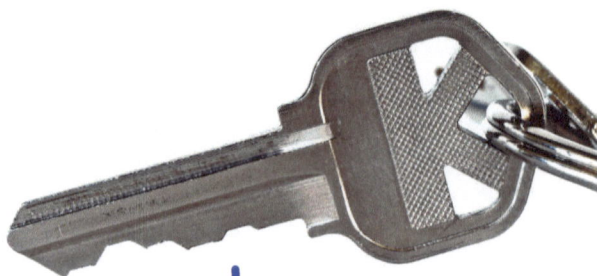

key

karate

Keep on thinking Kk!

Before you go to first grade, you go to
k _ _ _ _ _ _ _ _ _ _ _ _ .

Before you go to bed, you get a good-night
k _ _ _ .

To play soccer, you must learn to k _ _ _ the ball.

Only **one** of these two pictures begins with the Kk sound. Which one?

Which of these begins with the Kk sound?

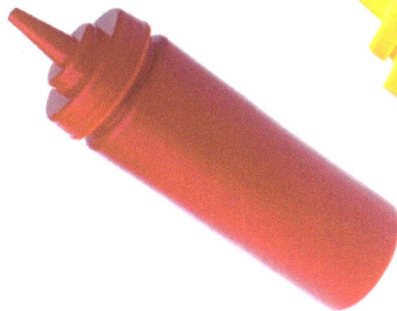

ANSWERS: kindergarten; kiss; kick; kitten; ketchup

Ll |||||

lamp

ladybug

ladder

lemon

lamb

leaf

Look carefully!

Which picture **does not** begin with the Ll sound?

Opposites! They all begin with the Ll sound.

What is the opposite of big?

What is the opposite of dark?

What is the opposite of early?

What is the opposite of short?

Which fruit begins with the Ll sound?

ANSWERS: mouse; little; light; late; long; lemon

Mm mmmmmm

milk

mouse

mug

mustard

money

mittens

Many other words begin with the Mm sound —

Where does the mailman put your mail?

You should never chew with your m _ _ _ _ open.

What shines in the sky at night?

What do you put on top of hot chocolate?

What do you put in a piggy bank?

ANSWERS: mailbox; mouth; moon; marshmallows; money

Nn
nnnnnn

nails

nest

napkin

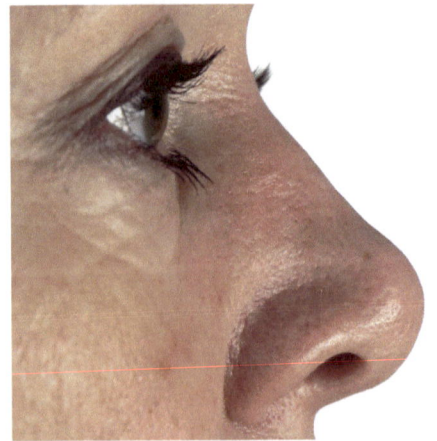

nose

numbers

Now for more about Nn —

Which number begins with Nn? 7, 8, 9, 10

What coin is worth 5 cents?

When do you see stars in the sky?

When do pigs fly?

What does it cost to walk to school?

Are you 6 feet tall?

This snowman has
a carrot for a n _ _ _ .

ANSWERS: nine (9); nickel; night; never; nothing; no; nose

Pp

as in paper

pie

peach

pig

puppy

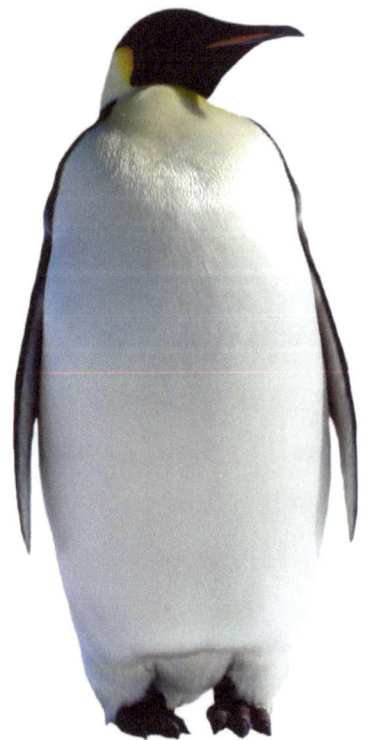

penguin

Perhaps you can think of more words that begin with the **Pp** sound —

If you poke a balloon with a pin, it will **p _ _** .

If you're riding in a wagon, someone has to **p _ _ _** or **p _ _ _ _** .

A fun place to play is in a **p _ _ _ _** .

To make a jack-o-lantern, you have to have a **p _ _ _ _ _ _ _** .

Which animal begins with the **Pp** sound?

Which food begins with the **Pp** sound?

ANSWERS: pop; pull, push; park; pumpkin; porcupine; pancakes

Qq

queen

quilt

quarters

quiet

The letter **Qq** usually has a partner, the letter u.
Qu is most often pronounced as kw.

Quickly see which answers you know!

What does a duck say? A duck says qu _ _ _ _ .

?

"Why?" is a qu _ _ _ _ _ _ _ .

Milk comes in pints, qu _ _ _ _ _ and gallons.

If you want someone to stop what they're doing, you might say, "Qu _ _ !"

ANSWERS: quack; question; quarts; quit

Rr rrrrrr

rabbit

rose

radishes

ring

rope

Rr you ready?

What is the missing **Rr** word —

Randy can **r** _ _ really fast.

Can you guess the answer to a **r** _ _ _ _ _ _ ?

You can see cowboys and horses at
a **r** _ _ _ _ _ .

Sometimes after a rain you see a
colorful **r** _ _ _ _ _ _ _ .

Which picture begins with the **Rr** sound?

ANSWERS: run; riddle; rodeo; rainbow; rocking chair

Ss
sssss

salt

sandwich

syrup

soccer ball

soap

sunglasses

See some more about the Ss sound —

Which animal begins with the **Ss** sound?

Which numbers begin with the **Ss** sound?

5, 6, 7, 8

Which would you put on a pancake? It begins with the **Ss** sound.

ANSWERS: seal; six and seven; syrup

Tt

as in two and ten

tomato

turtle or tortoise

tulips

tiger

Take a look at more words that begin with the Tt sound:

Something very, very small is t_ _ _ _ .

If you love your pet, you would never pull its t_ _ _ _ .

Someone who helps you learn in school is a t_ _ _ _ _ _ _ _ .

The number after nine is t_ _ _ .

Which picture begins with the Tt sound?

Which day of the week begins with the Tt sound?

What do you have on your feet that you can wiggle, and how many do you have?

ANSWERS: tiny; tail; teacher; ten;
turtle or tortoise; Tuesday; toes, ten

Vv

vvvvvv

Valentine

vegetables

volcano

violin

vine

Very important words

I don't just love you, I love you v _ _ _ much.

Remember to use your inside v _ _ _ _ _ .

She is using her outside v _ _ _ _ _ .

Summer is v _ _ _ _ _ _ _ _ time!

You might go v _ _ _ _ someone.

Ww as in wagon

watermelon

waffles

window

watch

wasp

Want more Ww?

What is in this bottle? It starts with the **Ww** sound.

What do you do to your hands before you eat?

You step on scales to see how much you **w** _ _ _ _ _ .

What do you make before you blow out your birthday candles?   You make a **w** _ _ _ .

What makes the leaves on trees move?

Which picture begins with the **Ww** sound?

ANSWERS: water; wash; weigh; wish; wind; wagon

Xx

X just says its name in **x**-ray:

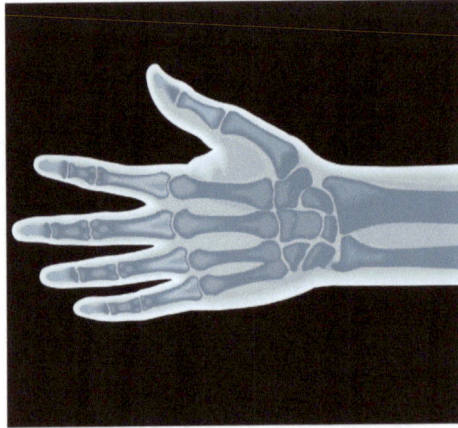

Sometimes it sounds like ks:

Sometimes it sounds like a **z** as in **x**ylophone:

Yy as in you

yoyos   **y**ell   **y**ogurt

What is the day before today?

You are talking to me and I am talking to **y** _ _ .

Sometimes when you're sleepy, you **y** _ _ _ .

ANSWERS: yesterday; you; yawn

Zz zzzzzz

zebra   **z**ipper   **z**ero

Say the name of the picture, then find its beginning sound.

Mm

Bb

Hh

Dd

Ss

Pp

Vowels

The vowels — **Aa**, **Ee**, **Ii**, **Oo**, **Uu** — have more than two pronunciations each; but only two, the long and short, are included here.

The letter **Yy** sometimes acts as a vowel, as in why, by, try, gym, hymn, gypsy, lazy, softly, only and many more words.

Aa

Sometimes **Aa** says its name, as in —

acorn

April

b**a**seball

pl**a**te

b**a**by

Sometimes **Aa** has a short sound, as in —

apple

abacus

r**a**bbit

l**a**dder

n**a**pkin

Ee

Sometimes **Ee** says its name, as in —

eagle

electric outlet

b**ee**

tr**ee**

s**ea**l

Sometimes **Ee** has a short sound, as in —

envelope

eggs

bed

tent

Ii

Sometimes **Ii** says its name, as in —

ice

ice cream

bike

tiger

pie

Sometimes **Ii** has a short sound, as in —

igloo

inch worm

pig

pitcher

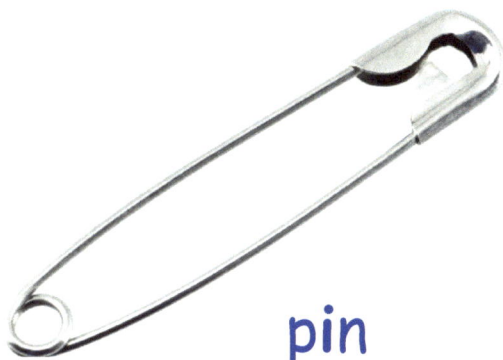

pin

Oo

Sometimes **Oo** says its name, as in —

open

ocean

g**o**at

y**o**y**o**s

b**o**w

r**o**se

Sometimes **Oo** has a short sound, as in —

olives

ostrich

rocks

socks

box

pot

Uu

Sometimes **Uu** says its name, as in —

uniform

ukulele

bugle

music

Sometimes **Uu** has a short sound, as in —

umbrella

underwear

d**u**cks

p**u**ppy

n**u**mbers

Can you match the picture with its beginning sound?

Aa

Ee

Ii

Oo

Uu

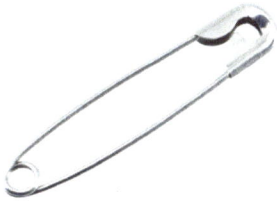

Can you
match
the picture
with
its name?

Say the
picture's
name.
Then
point to
the word
that says
its name.

hat

pig

cup

bed

dog

pot

pin

About the Author: Peggy L. Forster

Peggy Loud Forster is a native Oklahoman now living in San Francisco by way of Houston, Texas.

Her interest in teaching young children began when she realized the office job she had held for five years was pleasant but not fulfilling, while the volunteer work she had done with children was immensely satisfying. So, at age thirty she went back to the University of Oklahoma to earn her degree in Elementary Education.

Her teaching career began in Houston, teaching first grade, and ended in 1993, having taught second, third, and fourth grades as well. During that time she married, had two children, and was a stay-at-home mom for twelve years.

Eight years after retiring from teaching she began her new career as a grandmother, daughter Diane providing four grandchildren (of which Gavin is one) in Texas, and son David, one in California.

Her new career is shaping up to be the most fulfilling!

Acknowledgments

Grateful acknowledgment to those who taught me how to turn a scrappy-looking, would-be work-book into an appealing **work-with** book:

Korkor Apo — Artist, organizer, and computer genius who taught me the computer skills I needed as I needed them.

Mary Robinson — Long-time pre-kindergarten school teacher and past Owner/Director of Snell's Pre-Kindergarten School who taught me to see the pages through the eyes of a 4- or 5-year-old.

Linda Honeyman — Teacher of teachers, children, and adults of every age, who took the book to the field for a test run and advised me accordingly.

Emily Smith — Head of The Branch School in Houston, Texas, who really brought home the worth of "work-with."

Barbara Stopp Vance — for the final editing. Twenty-five years as a children's librarian in Round Rock, Texas, wired her to know how children think and talk and look at books.

In memory of Donna Johnson, past Owner/Director of Snell's Pre-Kindergarten School in Stockton, California, who saw this book as an answer to "How can I help my child?"

And my many friends who responded to the daily prompt, "How many nouns can you think of that begin with . . . ?"